NEVER LOSE YOUR SPARKLE

An Hachette UK Company
www.hachette.co.uk

Summersdale Publishers Ltd
Part of Octopus Publishing Group Limited
Carmelite House
50 Victoria Embankment
LONDON
EC4Y 0DZ
UK

www.summersdale.com

Printed and bound in Malta

ISBN: 978-1-84953-957-9

Substantial discounts on bulk quantities of Summersdale books are available to corporations, professional associations and other organisations. For details contact general enquiries: telephone: +44 (0) 1243 771107 email: enquiries@summersdale.com.

TO Karen – my friend
Love,
FROM Di xx

Keep smiling, because life is beautiful and there's so much to smile about.

MARILYN MONROE

Energy and persistence
conquer all things.

BENJAMIN FRANKLIN

Put your future in good
hands – your own.

ANONYMOUS

The more we do, the
more we can do.

WILLIAM HAZLITT

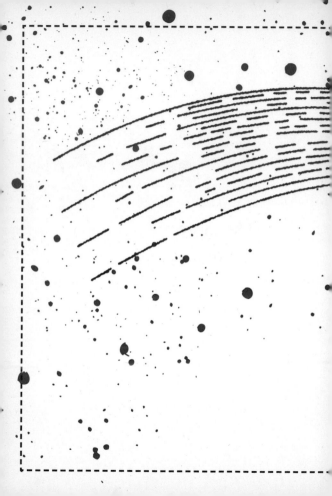

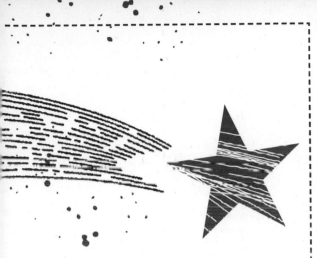

A SMILE IS A
CURVE THAT SETS
EVERYTHING STRAIGHT.

PHYLLIS DILLER

Every day brings a chance for you to draw in a breath, kick off your shoes, and dance.

OPRAH WINFREY

You are never too old
to set another goal or to
dream a new dream.

LES BROWN

Nothing is impossible,
the word itself says
'I'm possible'!

AUDREY HEPBURN

You protect your being
when you love yourself
better. That's the secret.

ISABELLE ADJANI

GO THE EXTRA MILE.
IT'S NEVER CROWDED.

It is never too late to be
what you might have been.

ADELAIDE ANNE PROCTER

Optimism is essential to achievement and it is also the foundation of courage.

NICHOLAS MURRAY BUTLER

Cherish forever what makes
you unique, 'cuz you're
really a yawn if it goes.

BETTE MIDLER

To accomplish great things,
we must not only act,
but also dream; not only
plan but also believe.

ANATOLE FRANCE

WHATEVER THE MIND OF
MAN CAN CONCEIVE AND
BELIEVE, IT CAN ACHIEVE.

NAPOLEON HILL

Believe in life!
Always human beings will
live and progress to greater,
broader, and fuller life.

W. E. B. DU BOIS

Why not just live in
the moment, especially
if it has a good beat?

GOLDIE HAWN

If you ask me what I came
into this life to do, I will tell
you: I came to live out loud.

ÉMILE ZOLA

It's never too late – never
too late to start over, never
too late to be happy.

JANE FONDA

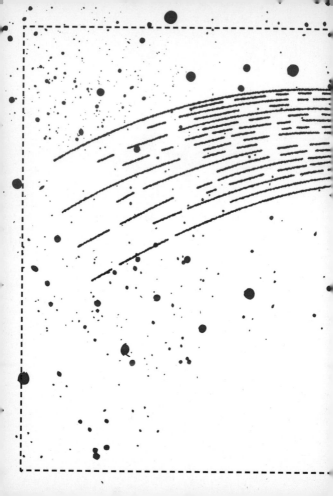

MAY YOU LIVE EVERY DAY
OF YOUR LIFE.

JONATHAN SWIFT

What we see depends mainly
on what we look for.

JOHN LUBBOCK

Every man is the architect
of his own fortune.

CAECUS

Just be yourself, there
is no one better.

TAYLOR SWIFT

If we all did the things we are capable of, we would literally astound ourselves.

THOMAS EDISON

ACT AS IF WHAT
YOU DO MAKES A
DIFFERENCE. IT DOES.

WILLIAM JAMES

Shoot for the moon.
Even if you fail you'll
land among the stars.

LES BROWN

Remember,
no matter where you
go, there you are.

CONFUCIUS

The outward man is the
swinging door; the inner
man is the still hinge.

MEISTER ECKHART

You have the answer. Just
get quiet enough to hear it.

PAT OBUCHOWSKI

YOUR SOUL IS ALL THAT
YOU POSSESS. TAKE IT
IN HAND AND MAKE
SOMETHING OF IT!

MARTIN H. FISCHER

We are sure to be losers
when we quarrel with
ourselves; it is civil war.

CHARLES CALEB COLTON

We have to dare to
be ourselves, however
frightening or strange that
self may prove to be.

MAY SARTON

Life is a pure flame, and we live by an invisible sun within us.

THOMAS BROWNE

Be thine own palace, or
the world's thy jail.

JOHN DONNE

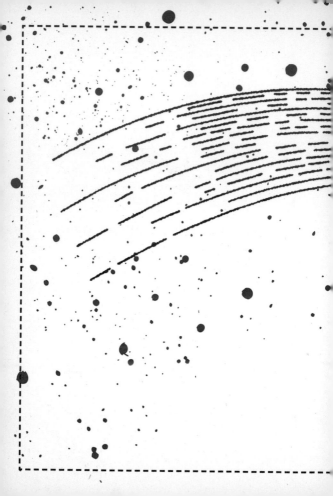

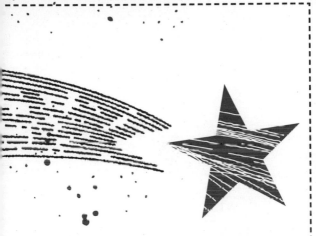

JUST THROW AWAY ALL
THOUGHTS OF IMAGINARY
THINGS, AND STAND FIRM
IN THAT WHICH YOU ARE.

KABIR

A wise man never loses
anything if he has himself.

MICHEL DE MONTAIGNE

What we do flows
from who we are.

PAUL VITALE

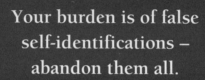

Your burden is of false
self-identifications –
abandon them all.

NISARGADATTA MAHARAJ

If you can't feed a
hundred people, then
just feed one.

MOTHER TERESA

NO ONE CAN DRIVE
US CRAZY UNLESS WE
GIVE THEM THE KEYS.

DOUGLAS HORTON

It's easy to get lost when
the map is in your hand
and not in your heart.

TERRI GUILLEMETS

Dig within. There lies the well-spring of good: ever dig, and it will ever flow.

MARCUS AURELIUS

Take the time
to come home to
yourself every day.

ROBIN CASARJIAN

The only person you
should ever compete with
is yourself. You can't hope
for a fairer match.

TODD RUTHMAN

WE MUST BE OUR
OWN BEFORE WE CAN
BE ANOTHER'S.

RALPH WALDO EMERSON

Always be a first-rate version
of yourself, instead of a second-
rate version of somebody else.

JUDY GARLAND

It takes courage to
grow up and become
who you really are.

E. E. CUMMINGS

Accept no one's
definition of your life;
define yourself.

HARVEY FIERSTEIN

There is just one life for
each of us: our own.

EURIPIDES

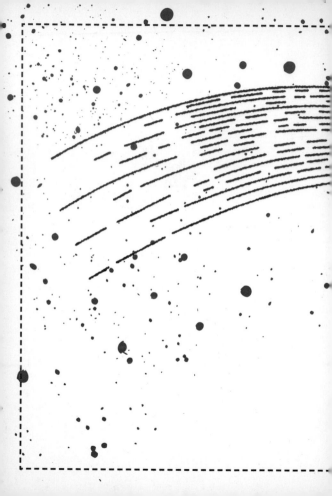

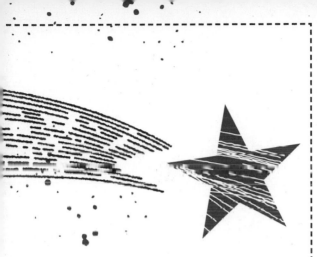

IF YOU'RE GOING TO
DOUBT SOMETHING,
DOUBT YOUR LIMITS.

DON WARD

When one is pretending
the entire body revolts.

ANAÏS NIN

Those who mind don't matter and those who matter don't mind.

BERNARD BARUCH

It is the chiefest point of happiness that a man is willing to be what he is.

DESIDERIUS ERASMUS

The most important
kind of freedom is to be
what you really are.

JIM MORRISON

WHAT I AM IS GOOD
ENOUGH IF I WOULD
ONLY BE IT OPENLY.

CARL ROGERS

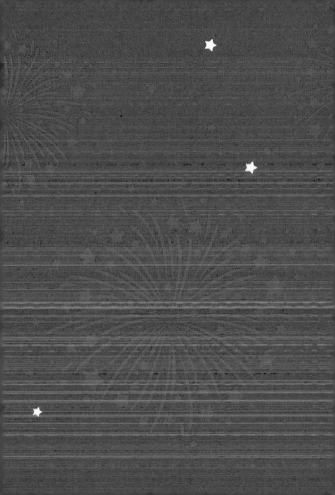

You were born an original.
Don't die a copy.

JOHN MASON

Who looks outside,
dreams. Who looks
inside, awakes.

CARL JUNG

The pen that writes your
life story must be held
in your own hand.

IRENE C. KASSORLA

Dare to be honest and
fear no labour.

ROBERT BURNS

DON'T LIVE DOWN TO
EXPECTATIONS. GO
OUT THERE AND DO
SOMETHING REMARKABLE.

WENDY WASSERSTEIN

Wheresoever you go,
go with all your heart.

CONFUCIUS

The best thing to hold on to in life is each other.

AUDREY HEPBURN

I am not a has-been.
I am a will be.

LAUREN BACALL

Always act like
you're wearing an
invisible crown.

ANONYMOUS

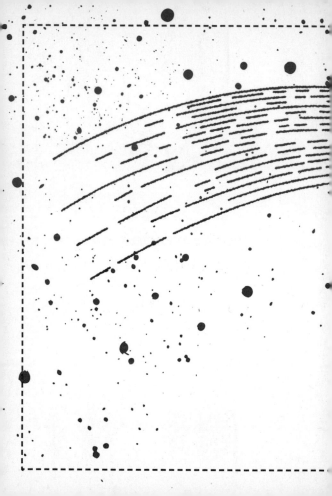

YOUR TIME IS LIMITED, SO
DON'T WASTE IT LIVING
SOMEONE ELSE'S LIFE.

STEVE JOBS

If I am not for myself,
then who will be for me?

HILLEL THE ELDER

The mould of a man's
fortune is in his own hands.

FRANCIS BACON

Do the best you can
until you know better.
Then when you know
better, do better.

MAYA ANGELOU

You don't get
harmony when everybody
sings the same note.

ANONYMOUS

ONE WHO WALKS IN
ANOTHER'S TRACKS
LEAVES NO FOOTPRINTS.

PROVERB

I may not be
different, but I'm
definitely not the same.

ANONYMOUS

Very little is needed to make a happy life; it is all within yourself, in your way of thinking.

MARCUS AURELIUS

Don't let them tame you.

ISADORA DUNCAN

If you obey all the rules
you miss all the fun.

KATHARINE HEPBURN

AS THE SCULPTOR DEVOTES
HIMSELF TO WOOD AND
STONE, I WOULD DEVOTE
MYSELF TO MY SOUL.

TOYOHIKO KAGAWA

Trust that little voice in your head that says, 'Wouldn't it be interesting if...' And then do it.

DUANE MICHALS

To unpathed waters,
undreamed shores.

WILLIAM SHAKESPEARE

When patterns are broken,
new worlds emerge.

TULI KUPFERBERG

My childhood may
be over but that doesn't
mean playtime is.

RON OLSON

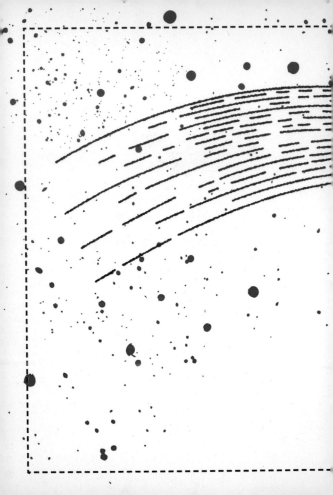

NEVER VIOLATE THE SACREDNESS OF YOUR INDIVIDUAL SELF-RESPECT.

THEODORE PARKER

Respect yourself and
others will respect you.

CONFUCIUS

Nobody made a greater
mistake than he who
did nothing because he
could only do a little.

EDMUND BURKE

Your spirit is
the true shield.

MORIHEI UESHIBA

Nobody can do
everything, but everyone
can do something.

ANONYMOUS

WHAT LIES BEHIND
YOU AND WHAT LIES IN
FRONT OF YOU, PALES IN
COMPARISON TO WHAT
LIES INSIDE OF YOU.

RALPH WALDO EMERSON

If you think you are too small
to be effective, you have never
been in bed with a mosquito.

DALAI LAMA

Don't count your days;
make your days count.

ANONYMOUS

In order to be
irreplaceable one must
always be different.

COCO CHANEL

If you keep doing things
like you've always done
them, what you'll get is
what you've already got.

ANONYMOUS

DON'T FORGET TO LOVE YOURSELF.

SØREN KIERKEGAARD

To help yourself you
must be yourself.

DAVE PELZER

To be yourself in a world that is constantly trying to make you something else is the greatest accomplishment.

RALPH WALDO EMERSON

Respect your efforts, respect yourself. Self-respect leads to self-discipline. When you have both firmly under your belt, that's real power.

CLINT EASTWOOD

If you don't know what you're here to do, then just do some good.

MAYA ANGELOU

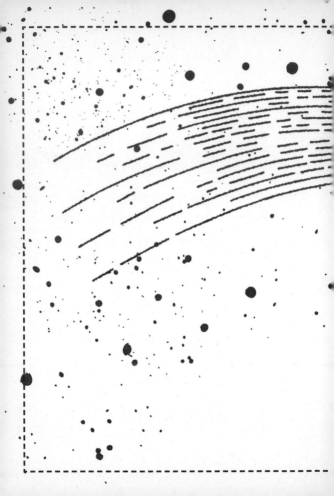

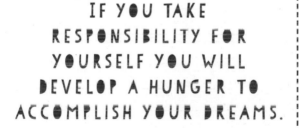

IF YOU TAKE
RESPONSIBILITY FOR
YOURSELF YOU WILL
DEVELOP A HUNGER TO
ACCOMPLISH YOUR DREAMS.

LES BROWN

Have patience with all things,
but first of all with yourself.

FRANCIS DE SALES

Don't be 'consistent',
but be simply true.

OLIVER WENDELL HOLMES SR

Don't be a blueprint.
Be an original.

ROY ACUFF

To be awake is
to be alive.

HENRY DAVID THOREAU

TRUST YOURSELF. YOU
KNOW MORE THAN
YOU THINK YOU DO.

BENJAMIN SPOCK

Why fit in when you were
born to stand out?

DR. SEUSS

Your big opportunity
may be right where
you are now.

NAPOLEON HILL

With self-discipline, most anything is possible.

THEODORE ROOSEVELT

A strong, positive self-image is the best possible preparation for success.

JOYCE BROTHERS

THE LIMITS OF POSSIBLE
CAN ONLY BE DEFINED
BY GOING BEYOND THEM
INTO THE IMPOSSIBLE.

ARTHUR C. CLARKE

This above all: to thine
own self be true.

WILLIAM SHAKESPEARE

Success in any endeavour depends on the degree to which it is an expression of your true self.

RALPH MARSTON

Beauty is when you can appreciate yourself. When you love yourself, that's when you're most beautiful.

ZOË KRAVITZ

Believe you can and
you're halfway there.

THEODORE ROOSEVELT

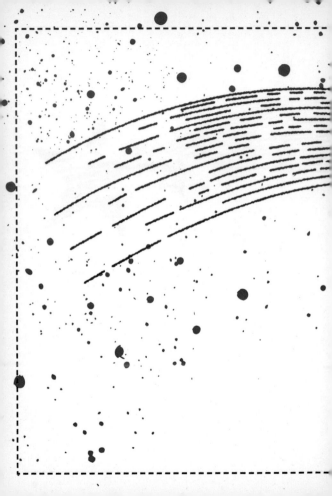

SELF-TRUST IS THE FIRST SECRET OF SUCCESS.

RALPH WALDO EMERSON

Know and believe in
yourself, and what others
think won't disturb you.

WILLIAM FEATHER

Be brave enough to
live creatively… what
you discover will be
wonderful. What you
discover will be yourself.

ALAN ALDA

Yes, know thyself: in great concerns or small,
Be this thy care, for this,
my friend, is all.

JUVENAL

Follow your honest
convictions, and stay strong.

WILLIAM MAKEPEACE THACKERAY

IMAGINATION IS THE HIGHEST KITE ONE CAN FLY.

ANONYMOUS

Be yourself; everyone
else is already taken.

OSCAR WILDE

Be not afraid of
growing slowly; be afraid
only of standing still.

CHINESE PROVERB

Knowing yourself is the
beginning of all wisdom.

ARISTOTLE

Our ideas, like
orange-plants, spread out in
proportion to the size of the
box which imprisons the roots.

EDWARD BULWER-LYTTON

WHAT PROGRESS, YOU
ASK, HAVE I MADE? I
HAVE BEGUN TO BE A
FRIEND TO MYSELF.

HECATO

Put your ear down
close to your soul
and listen hard.

ANNE SEXTON

Human potential is the
only limitless resource
we have in this world.

CARLY FIORINA

When you do things from
your soul you feel a river
moving in you, a joy.

RUMI

The most powerful
weapon on earth is the
human soul on fire.

FERDINAND FOCH

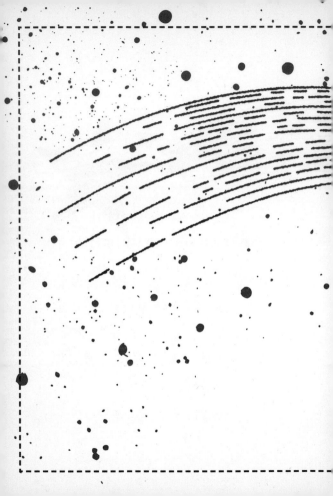

DARE TO BE DIFFERENT
AND TO SET YOUR OWN
PATTERN, LIVE YOUR OWN
LIFE AND FOLLOW YOUR
OWN STAR.

WILFRED PETERSON

It is not wrong to be different. Sometimes it is hard, but it is not wrong.

ELIZABETH MOON

Being your true self is the
most effective formula
for success there is.

DANIELLE LAPORTE

The spirit is the true self.
The spirit, the will to win,
and the will to excel, are
the things that endure.

CICERO

There is but one
cause of human failure.
And that is man's lack of
faith in his true self.

WILLIAM JAMES

BE CONGRUENT, BE AUTHENTIC, BE YOUR TRUE SELF.

MAHATMA GANDHI

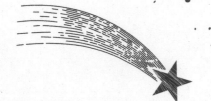

If you're interested in finding out
more about our books, find us on
Facebook at **Summersdale Publishers**
and follow us on Twitter at **@Summersdale**.

www.summersdale.com